MIX
Papier aus verantwortungsvollen Quellen
Paper from responsible sources
FSC® C105338

Tan Kwan Hong

The Future of Rural Banking in China

A Pragmatic Discourse on Current Issues, with Policy Recommendations for the Future

Anchor Academic Publishing

Kwan Hong, Tan: The Future of Rural Banking in China. A Pragmatic Discourse on
Current Issues, with Policy Recommendations for the Future, Hamburg, Anchor
Academic Publishing 2016

Buch-ISBN: 978-3-96067-032-2
PDF-eBook-ISBN: 978-3-96067-532-7
Druck/Herstellung: Anchor Academic Publishing, Hamburg, 2016
Covermotiv: © pixabay.de

Bibliografische Information der Deutschen Nationalbibliothek:
Die Deutsche Nationalbibliothek verzeichnet diese Publikation in der Deutschen
Nationalbibliografie; detaillierte bibliografische Daten sind im Internet über
http://dnb.d-nb.de abrufbar.

Bibliographical Information of the German National Library:
The German National Library lists this publication in the German National Bibliography.
Detailed bibliographic data can be found at: http://dnb.d-nb.de

All rights reserved. This publication may not be reproduced, stored in a retrieval system
or transmitted, in any form or by any means, electronic, mechanical, photocopying,
recording or otherwise, without the prior permission of the publishers.

Das Werk einschließlich aller seiner Teile ist urheberrechtlich geschützt. Jede Verwertung
außerhalb der Grenzen des Urheberrechtsgesetzes ist ohne Zustimmung des Verlages
unzulässig und strafbar. Dies gilt insbesondere für Vervielfältigungen, Übersetzungen,
Mikroverfilmungen und die Einspeicherung und Bearbeitung in elektronischen Systemen.

Die Wiedergabe von Gebrauchsnamen, Handelsnamen, Warenbezeichnungen usw. in
diesem Werk berechtigt auch ohne besondere Kennzeichnung nicht zu der Annahme,
dass solche Namen im Sinne der Warenzeichen- und Markenschutz-Gesetzgebung als frei
zu betrachten wären und daher von jedermann benutzt werden dürften.

Die Informationen in diesem Werk wurden mit Sorgfalt erarbeitet. Dennoch können
Fehler nicht vollständig ausgeschlossen werden und die Diplomica Verlag GmbH, die
Autoren oder Übersetzer übernehmen keine juristische Verantwortung oder irgendeine
Haftung für evtl. verbliebene fehlerhafte Angaben und deren Folgen.

Alle Rechte vorbehalten

© Anchor Academic Publishing, Imprint der Diplomica Verlag GmbH
Hermannstal 119k, 22119 Hamburg
http://www.diplomica-verlag.de, Hamburg 2016
Printed in Germany

Table of Contents

Section 1: Abstract	4
Section 2: Past Issues in Rural Banking	7
Section 3: Past Reforms on China's Rural Banking Sector	10
Section 4: Unsolved and New, Emerging Issues from the Post-Reform Era	16
Section 5: Other Goals of the Chinese Government	32
Section 6: The Other Commonly Forgotten Goal – Increasing the Relevance of the Rural Banking Sector	33
Section 7: Rural Banking Sector Reforms for a Brighter Future	34
Section 8: Conclusion	54

The Future of Rural Banking in China

Section 1: Abstract

Described by Nicholas Lardy as the "Unfinished Economic Revolution"[1], the path of financial sector reforms in rural areas in China, which holds the country's massive savings, has been a rocky one.

Further, given the importance of China as the world's second largest economy and the prominent role of her banking sector, analyzing the current state and future of the rural banking sector is of great interest.

The importance of this paper is given further weight, given that three-quarters of the country's population still reside in rural areas, since the Communist revolution in 1949. These people, which forms the majority of the population in China, has been served by The Rural Credit Cooperatives (RCCs), or nongcun xinyong hezuoshe, which have been the core credit institutions in rural China.

However, despite her major role in rural economic development, and the direct role in influencing the standards of living and well-being of her rural dwellers, the RCCs has proven to be less than an effective mechanism in appropriate resource allocation and effective loan generation.

Issues such as agency problems and the collective action problem, their causes and implications, will be discussed in detail in this report.

Those problems aside, the RCCs, like other government or quasi-government organizations in China, are heavily influenced by Communist Party institutions at the local level. Local Party committees frequently interfere in credit institutions' loan allocations to favor their enterprises and projects, in order to promote the local economic growth on which their political careers depend.

Such a policy has larger than expected consequences in the entire rural financial system, and this will also be discussed in the report.

This paper therefore provides a vital attempt in constructing the future of rural banking in China. The authors attempt to address this topic in a pragmatic approach, by considering the present ills of the current system and the future solutions and policies that can be used to improve the entire system as a whole.

Through a pragmatic and policy-like approach on this topic, the improvements made to the rural commercial banking system via the recommended policies will potentially positively impact the lives of millions, spurring rapid economic growth and decreasing the widening income disparity between urban and rural dwellers.

But just like how a doctor needs to know a patient's medical history in order to find the correct diagnostics or medication for her future good health, the authors too, in the midst of the project, realized an ardent need to do additional research and analysis on past reforms of the rural banking systems in China.

It is at this point that we realize the importance of the configuration of the Communist Party's power in these financial organizations. Based on our literature reviews on this topic, we realized that a majority of researchers studying China's financial systems have tended to treat the Communist Party's influence as non-existent or something exogenous to the system, perhaps due to a lack of assess to valuable data. Notable exceptions are Heilmann, who looks at policymaking and institutional politics in Shanghai's financial industry[2], and Shih, who deals with elite politics in the banking industry[3]. However, the party's influence over the financial organizations is so great that it must be a focus for analysis. Apart from some work on the party's influence on the corporate governance of state-holding corporations[4] and on cadre management[5], how Party institutions operate and how they exert authority in financial organizations is almost a "black box" to the Western world. As this paper will establish, unraveling this "black box" is crucial in getting to the crux of the issue.

Extending this line of analysis, this paper examines the extent to which the most recent institutional reforms have addressed the effects of insider control, the problem of collective action for member households, and the influence of the local Party on the operations of the rural credit organizations.

After a detailed analysis of the past reforms and issues of the rural commercial banking industry, and in the role of the Communist Party towards the industry, towards the later sections of the paper, we highlight the objectives that the future of rural banking industry in China must achieve for more effective resource allocation, and for the betterment of the rural community.

It is at this juncture that the authors also realized that in order to meet these meaningful objectives, active efforts in reforms have to be made in entities and best practices that go way beyond the rural banking industry.

For easy reading, this paper is structured as follows:

Section 1: Abstract
Section 2: Past Issues in Rural Banking
Section 3: Past Reforms on China's Rural Banking Sector
Section 4: Unsolved and New, Emerging Issues from the Post-Reform Era
Section 5: Other Goals of the Chinese Government
Section 6: The Other Commonly Forgotten Goal – Increasing the Relevance of the Rural Banking Sector
Section 7: Rural Banking Sector Reforms for a Brighter Future
Section 8: Conclusion

Section 2: Past Issues in Rural Banking

Since the Communist revolution in 1949, the Rural Credit Cooperatives (RCCs), or nongcun xinyong hezuoshe, have been the core credit institutions in rural China, where three-quarters of the country's population still reside.

Despite being the only formal credit organization with a network extending to the grassroots level (also known as the townships), the RCCs are the major – and usually the sole – formal providers of much-needed credit to rural households. Unfortunately, the RCCs are not very effective in meeting the credit demands of the very constituencies that they are supposed to serve. Rural households consistently contribute more than 80 percent of total deposits[6], but account for only one-third of total loans. Moreover, all thanks to the nonperforming loans granted to township and village enterprises (TVEs), RCCs became ridden with mountains of bad debt[7]. This largely deprives the credit cooperatives of valuable funds for loans, therefore further reducing the supply of credit to rural households.

On top and beyond the issues of nonperforming loans, other problems such as "agency problems" and collective action problems exist within the system. This has got to do with the fact that these credit organizations were being nominally "cooperatives", which refers to organizations that are owned, managed and operated by members and designed to serve their needs.

In organizational analysis, "agency problems" are usually unavoidable when there is a separation of both the ownership and management functions[8]. When the principal (owner) and agent (manager) have divergent objectives, the agent could pursue his own personal interest at the expense of the inherent interests of the principal. In the case of the RCCs, because member households seldom take part in member representative meetings, the manager holds an informational advantage that gives him huge control and power over the running of these credit institutions, resulting in insider control, an issue familiar in the literature on corporate governance.

Furthermore, member households face the collective action problem in monitoring the agent's behaviour[9]. This is a problem recognized in studies of corporate governance: being part of a large sample group of dispersed corporate shareholders, individual members have minimal personal incentive to monitor the agent's actions. The large number of rural households or depositors in a township credit cooperative—from 5,000 to 25,000 in the areas researched—means that any gains and benefits derived from any mobilized action will also accrue to those who do not invest any effort.

These are, unfortunately, not the only issues faced within the system. The RCCs, like other government or quasi-government organizations in China, are heavily influenced by Communist Party institutions at the local level. Local Party committees frequently interfere in credit institutions' loan-allocating decisions to benefit the enterprises and projects they oversee, so as to promote the much-needed local economic growth that will in turn affect their career advancements in the political circuit. Local Party committees influence the operation of rural credit organizations by exercising influence over cadre management or the nomenklatura system to which RCC senior management belong[10].

The interference of local government in the allocation of loans has significant implications for how the literature has traditionally perceived the role of local government. Many scholars have traditionally seen this role as beneficial in regard to the country's economic development, describing the local states as "corporatist" (Oi),[11] "entrepreneurial" (Duckett)[12] and "developmental" (Blecher and Shue).[13]

In various extents, these papers have given their support and approval for the local states for their interventionist and instrumental roles in rural industrialization. They perceive this activity as underpinning the wider economic expansion, on the grounds that fiscal decentralization, in giving local states an incentive to retain revenue, has prompted them to engage vigorously in income-generating business activities—put simply, to behave like "corporations" and "entrepreneurs."

Evidence highlighted in this study, however, calls for a fundamental reassessment of the role of local states. The mounting problem of the non-performing assets of rural credit cooperatives resulting from massive loans granted to local government-owned TVEs shows evidently the need to reassess the impacts of local government business-like behavior.

Section 3: Past Reforms on China's Rural Banking Sector

Three-quarters of China's population still resides in the countryside. Low-income rural residents in China relied heavily on their access to the formal credit market to maintain their basic livelihoods, while those in peri-urban areas depend on credit access to improve their living standards[14]. Since the early 1980s, the central government in China has been working to reform 35,000 Rural Credit Cooperatives (RCCs) nationwide—the mainstay of formal credit throughout rural China—to ensure that they are better able to serve the credit needs and demands of local communities. Despite various government policies to improve households' access to credit, a consistent feature of the RCCs is that their loans are often allocated to local government-owned enterprises and projects, rather than to rural households involved in either farming or small trading. Throughout the 1980s and 1990s, loans to local government-owned collective enterprises consistently accounted for about half of the RCC loans, leaving the rural households with a quarter or less, despite the fact that more than 80 percent of the RCCs' capital has consistently come from the savings of rural households, as indicated in the Almanac of China's Finance and Banking (Zhongguo Jinrong Nianjian) (see figures 1 and 2 for details).

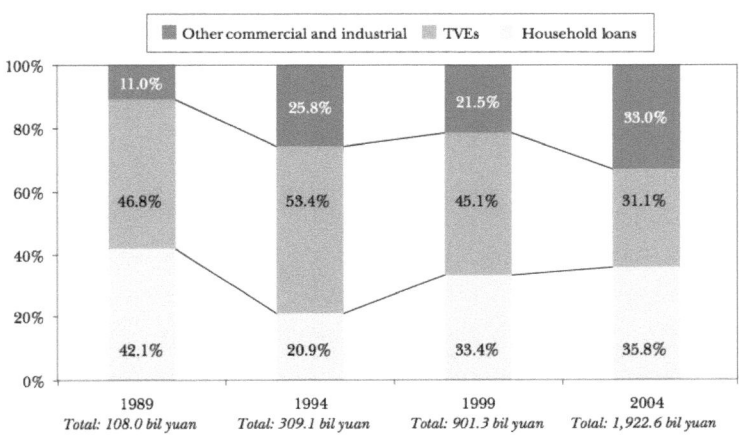

Figure 1
Composition of RCCs' Loans Nationwide (Various Years)

Communist Party and Financial Institutions in China

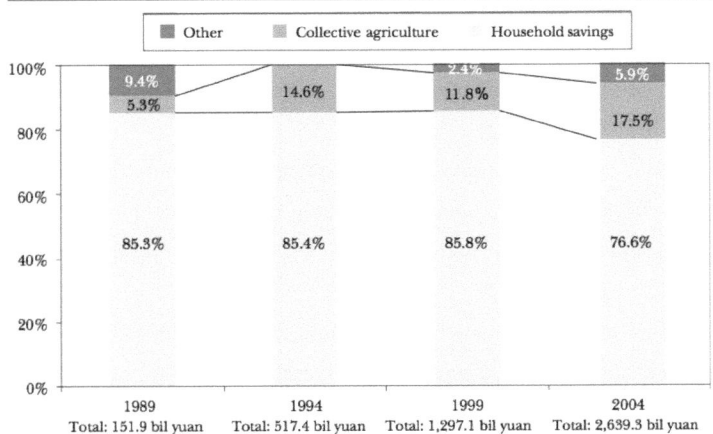

Figure 2
Composition of RCCs' Savings Nationwide (Various Years)

Because local government-related borrowers typically is a much higher contributor to default rates than household borrowers, the RCCs suffer chronic financial losses, and have to deal with mountains of bad debt; the non-performing loan (NPL) rate nationwide was estimated at 50 percent in the late 1990s[15]. The immense financial burdens have also drained the liquidity of these small credit organizations and constrained their ability to lend to households.

After Deng Xiaoping launched his market reforms in 1979, the central government made the RCCs report to a state-owned bank, the Agricultural Bank of China (ABC). These RCCs were previously subordinated to the rural communes. For the next 17 years, the RCCs functioned as grassroots branches of the state-owned bank, though they kept separate accounts, and their employees were awarded based on a different compensation system, which usually paled in comparison to their state-owned bank colleagues[16].

The RCCs formally parted ways with the Agricultural Bank of China in 1996 following an overhaul of the state-owned bank's operations. Instead, more county credit unions were set up by the central bank to manage grassroots cooperatives[17]. Since then central policymakers have been looking for a suitable institutional model for the RCCs to make them "truly accountable to member households" and to become "commercially sustainable."[18]

In June 2003, the central government implemented pilot reforms in eight places, which included Zhejiang, Jiangsu, Shandong, Jiangxi, Shaanxi, Guizhou and Jilin provinces, and Chongqing municipality. The major reform objectives included:

(a) Transfer of management rights (guanli quan) of the RCCs to the provincial governments, which are responsible for overseeing the RCC management, and are not to be involved directly in detailed operations.

(b) The RCCs can adopt an institutional model from a choice of three different models: the rural commercial banking model, the rural cooperative banking model and the original rural credit cooperatives model.

1. Localities with a higher degree of industrialization and a lesser need to support agricultural households can adopt the profit-maximizing commercial banking model.
2. Localities that still have disproportionately large numbers of subsistent households are to retain the original cooperative model.
3. Cooperative banks are suitable for those locales that are neither highly developed nor poor and subsistent.

The qualifying criteria for the models also differ in terms of financial performance of credit organizations, with the commercial banking model requiring the best performance, followed by the cooperative banking and the credit cooperative models, respectively[19].

The specifics of these models will be touched on later in the report.

To ease the RCCs of their financial difficulties, a variety of policies were implemented by the central bank to make the RCCs financially viable. For example, the largest ongoing aid programme is an interest-rate subsidy, under which the RCCs can loan funds from the central bank at around 2 percent and yield a handsome profit when the money is loaned to farmers at market interest rates.

In addition, the central bank also provided 30 billion yuan worth of subsidies to those credit cooperatives that suffered losses due to the central government's interest-guarantee policy in the period from 1994 to 1997[20].

The central government also decreased business tax (yingyeshui) and gave full exemptions to some credit cooperatives, especially those in the relatively poor central and western regions, exempting them from paying corporate income tax. The non-performing loans (NPLs) of the RCCs are largely made up of non-recovered loans to local government-related enterprises and projects.

From the perspective of the borrower, the mirror image of the NPLs is the mounting local government debt; primarily from township authorities that have relied most heavily on lending from the RCCs. Official figures suggest that at least half of the RCCs' aggregate NPLs of 515 billion yuan in 2002 were owed by local governments. The likelihood of local governments repaying these loans is slim, particularly in capital-strapped localities. Field research data in two poor counties in Sichuan suggests that township debts owed to RCCs range from 1.4 to 40 times the townships' annual fiscal revenues[21].

Hence, the central government's financial subsidies forming part of the recent reform package—168 billion yuan debt-for-bonds swaps and 930 million yuan earmarked central bank loans[22]—have both the effects of not only assisting the RCCs to dispose of their bad assets and historical losses, but also the effect of bailing out the local governments[23]. Further, according to the central bank's policy, the respective provincial governments are supposed to match the central government's 168 billion yuan contribution to clean up the RCCs' balance sheets[24].

Reforms of the rural credit cooperatives epitomize the complexity of China's political economy and highlight the obstacles with regard to financial-sector reforms[25]. Since the mid-1980s, the central government has planned new institutional design to make the credit organizations genuinely accountable to member households[26]. After separation from the state-owned bank in 1996 until 2003, the grassroots RCCs were loosely managed by central bank branches, predominantly at the provincial and county levels. The lack of strict vertical management structure made them easy targets for control by local governments.

Despite the large variety of financial institutions present in China, about half of the market is still controlled by the large state-owned banks. However, their market share has been decreasing over time. Competition increased with reforms as the large state-owned banks moved out of their traditional specializations and joint-stock banks were established (OECD, 2005). This development is mostly evident in urban areas as reforms caused commercial banks to largely withdraw from lending activities in rural areas in the late 1990s. Consequently, rural households were left with very limited access to credit. Comprehensive reform of the rural credit system was implemented starting from 2003 to improve this situation, and various types of institutions were established to serve the heterogeneous needs of rural borrowers.

To increase the quality of services and competition, foreign investors have also been encouraged to participate. Foreign investors in general expect the Chinese market to growth further, but it is an open question as to how much foreign banks will be able to increase market share as domestic banks become more competitive (OECD, 2010).

Section 4: Unsolved and New, Emerging Issues from the Post-Reform Era

In the post-reform era of rural banking and credit cooperatives in China, significant improvements can be seen from the organizational structure on how these credit organizations now operate. These improvements include a management and decision making structure that is more resistant to insider control, and one which promotes a greater diffusion of power among stakeholders, with more shared responsibilities. More check-and-balance mechanisms have also been placed.

However, it does present several other newly emerged corporate governance issues that we will address.

Institutional Design of the Post-Reform Rural Credit Organizations

Corporate Governance Structure

In a cooperative credit organization, the member representative meeting, made up of the ordinary members, is the highest governing body. In theory, members nominate and elect those who sit on the board of directors and board of supervisors; the supervisory board supervises the board of directors; and the head of the board of directors becomes the key decision maker[27].

Nonetheless, in the case of pre-reform RCCs, the member representative meeting (huiyuan daibiao dahui) consists of township- and village-leading cadres (lingdao ganbu), instead of the fee-paying members (rugu huiyuan). Out of a sample of about 300 member households, only 12 percent had ever attended a member representative meeting; these people, or their spouses, were, at that time, either township or village heads or secretaries[28]. The board of directors typically comprises only RCC officers, and is headed by the RCC manager. While the township

Party secretary typically leads the board of supervisors, the supervisory board comprises township cadres exclusively.

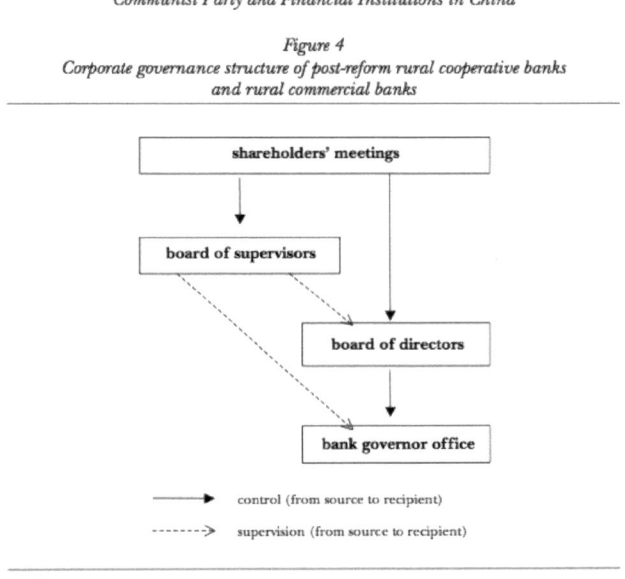

Figure 4
Corporate governance structure of post-reform rural cooperative banks and rural commercial banks

How has the corporate governance structure changed as a result of the institutional reform? As illustrated in figure 4, the corporate governance structure of the post-reform credit organizations consists of the board of directors, bank governor's office, board of supervisors and the shareholders' meeting.

Board of Directors (Dongshi hui)

During the post-reform era, the composition of the Board of Directors (BOD) differs among the three different credit organizations. In a typical scenario, the head of the BOD is both the credit organization's legal representative (faren daibiao) and the internal Party committee's secretary.

The RCCs that followed the original cooperative model made little changes in their BOD, which is made up of RCC employees. Compare this to the BOD in rural cooperative banks, which comprises of employee and non-employee member shareholders, with the number of the non-employees usually exceeding that of employees. The non-employee shareholders can be individual shareholders (geren gudong) or representatives of company shareholders (qiye gudong).

Comparing the BOD of the rural cooperative banks with that of the original cooperatives, the monopoly power of the credit organizations' employees, or insider control, has diminished considerably.

On top of having employee and non-employee shareholders that dilutes insider control, rural commercial banks also accept a number of independent directors on their board. These independent directors have no stake in the financial organizations and therefore are supposed to be impartial and unbiased, providing their long-term outlook at the same time. They are usually economics professors, successful entrepreneurs, or retired government officials familiar with banking operations who are invited to sit on the board to balance against the interests of those who hold shares in the organizations. Independent directors are appointed by the head of the BOD[29].

Bank Governor's Office (Hangzhang shi)

Previously, the bank governor's office does not exist in the original RCCs. It is a newly set-up institution within the frameworks of the rural cooperative banks and rural commercial banks. The BOD delegates the rights to the bank governor's office to make daily operational decisions. Before the reformation, the head of the BOD used to function both as the decision maker for strategic issues and day-to-day operations. However due to the new regulation of the rural commercial banks and rural cooperative banks, it specifically states that one cannot occupy both the positions of head of the BOD and bank governor. Furthermore, the previous over-concentrated power in the hands of an individual has been curbed in the new structure as this new regulation has been strictly followed.

With clear separation of functions between the head of the BOD and bank governor, loan approval decisions are now subject to more strict and stringent procedures by the loan approval committee. The loan approval committee operates under the bank governor's office and BOD. The decisions on big loans made by the loan approval committee have also fall outside the purview of branch managers[30]. It is noteworthy that these decisions used to be the exclusive privilege of the head of the BOD as mentioned above. Other than the loan approval committee, further various committees have been established under the BOD and the bank governor's office to institutionalize various decision-making processes. For example, in rural cooperative banks, there are basically three committees operating under the BOD: a risk management, personnel wage and audit committee. In addition, an internal transaction committee has been included. All these committees report directly to the board of directors.[31]

As mentioned of the audit committee, it is a desirable creation as it signifies the attempt of taking financial misconducts seriously. Though the effectiveness of such micro-organizations might still be far from clear at this stage, through the internal audits, they do reflect cases of fraud and financial crimes in the bank. Thus the importance of the audit committee can be shown as audit committees in some rural commercial banks are increasingly playing a more prominent role than in the past.[32]

Although the audit committee is playing a more prominent role now, it is still important to know the different functions between the audit committee and the Party disciplinary inspection committee (dangjilv jiancha weiyuan hui or jijianwei), as well as their relationship. Basically, when the audit found upon a financial misconduct in the professional aspect, it will be hand the relevant personnel over to the Party disciplinary inspection committee for action. However if the individuals are Party members, the committee will take action against them based on the Party disciplinary rules instead.[33] Hence, the final power of investigation still lies in the hands of the Party disciplinary inspection committee, though the existence of an audit committee means enhanced vigilance against financial misconduct.

Board of Supervisors (Jianshi hui)

In reality, BOS does not function exactly from what is stated in the organization charter. In practice, the effectiveness of the BOS is very limited and this is shown more in the case of the RCCs and rural cooperative banks than in the rural commercial banks. As compared in theory, members of BOS should be appointed in the shareholders' meeting and able to supervise the BOD and the bank governor office.[34]

What interests me more is that the post-reform rural credit organizations are using the same people as their bank executives, even before the reform. Usually there is change in the structure, for example the head of the BOD was the previous director of the county union (zhuren), the deputy head of the BOD was the deputy director (fu zhuren), and the head of the BOS was the office manager. Rarely any new blood is injected into the top management sector after reforms also reflects that there is a lack of qualified banking personnel in the localities. Thus in order to improve this situation, new qualified banking practitioners may be employed as the banks develop over time.[35]

The Collective Action Problem and Insider Control

Collective action problem is always one of the corporate governance problems faced in the original RCCs. Due to the high cost required in monitoring managers, the RCCs' member households results in a relatively weaker control over the RCCs' officers.[36] It is interesting to see how credit cooperative senior management perceives this problem. An internal document prepared by the head of the BOS[37] in a Zhejiang RCC notes that "because of the small number of shares owned by member households and members of the BOD and the BOS, they do no more than raise their hands and eat buns (jujuquantou, chichimantou) during meetings!"

To what extent has this problem been addressed by the institutional transformation? The RCCs that retain the original model have had little change in their share structures, even though the size of their capital base has expanded. Here, we compare the share structures of a pre- and post-reform rural cooperative bank and those of a rural commercial bank.[38] Generally, shares of rural cooperative banks are divided into "natural person" shares, (ziran rengu) owned by individuals including employees, and "legal person" shares (faren gu), simply means corporate shares which owned by companies. Each type of share has a basic "individual shares"[39] (zige gu), and the rest are "investment shares" (touzi gu).

The collective action problem still exists in the post-reform rural cooperative bank, though its degree may have diminished somewhat. The number of shareholders has reduced from 60,000 to 13,500; the shares are still rather thinly spread, with the top ten shareholders holding only slightly over 10 percent of total shares collectively. The largest shareholders are bank employees, with the single largest owning 1.5 percent of total shares. In fact, the banks' charters have imposed restrictions on maximum share ownership. A corporation and its related companies or the "legal person" can only hold a maximum of 0.5 percent of total shares, while bank employees and other "natural persons" can hold 1.5 and 0.5 percent, respectively. It is noteworthy that these restrictions are established in prevention of exerting excess control over the RCCs by those dominated large shareholders.[40]

With respect to insider control, despite the absence of pre-reform comparative data, employees, as a group, own a sizeable one-quarter share of the post-reform rural cooperative bank, as indicated in table 1. Given the large and dispersed nature of the bank's shareholders, bank employees are by far the single largest group of shareholders, indicating that insider control is still a thorny issue in the post-reform rural cooperative bank.

Table 1
Comparison of share structures between a pre- and post-reform rural cooperative bank

	Rural Cooperative Bank	Previously RCC
Number of members/shareholders	13,567	60,000
Total members'/shareholders' equity (yuan)	200 million, of which 155 million are "natural person" shares (55 million of which are held by employees) and 45 million are "legal person" shares	24.6 million
Shares held by employees (% of total)	50 million (25%)	N.A.
Voting rights	In addition to an "eligibility threshold" that is equivalent to one vote, for a "natural person" every additional 2,000 investment shares provides one extra vote; for a "legal person" every additional 20,000 shares provides one extra vote	One-person-one-vote
Maximum shares held (% of total shares)	"Natural person," including employees: 301,000 yuan (1.5%) "Legal person": 1.01 million (0.5%)	N.A.
Shares held by top 10 shareholders (% of total shares)	11.3%	N.A.
Number of representatives in members' representative meetings (% of total share)	75: 19 are employees (25%), 39 other "natural person" (52%), 17 "legal person" (23%)	N.A.

N.A.: not available or not applicable
Source: the rural cooperative bank's charter

Turning to the rural commercial bank, the collective action problem has diminished by a large extent after the institutional reform. As table 2 indicates, the number of shareholders fell from 120,000 to 1,656, and the top ten shareholders now hold more than one-third share in the rural commercial bank. Having a bigger stake in the commercial bank provides large shareholders greater incentive to monitor the manager's actions. Hence, everything else being equal, the collective action problem has been curtailed to a greater extent in the rural commercial bank than in the rural cooperative bank. Some may argue that dominance by large shareholders will hinder participation by small shareholders, but the amount of shares held by the top ten shareholders in the rural commercial bank (only one- third of the total) does not seem to be large enough to preclude participation by others.

Table 2
Comparison of share structures between a pre- and post-reform rural commercial bank

	Rural Commercial Bank	Previously RCC
Number of members/shareholders	1,656, consisting of 1,545 "natural persons" of whom 797 are employees and 111 are "legal persons"	120,000
Total members'/shareholders' equity (*yuan*)	315 million	14 million
Composition of shares (% *of total shares*)	"Natural persons": 161.9 million (*51.4%*) of which employees are 50.9 million (*16.95%*) "Legal persons": 153.1 million (*48.6%*)	"Employee": 7.9 million (*56.6%*) "Natural person": 2.9 million (*20.9%*) "Legal person": 3.2 million (*22.5%*)
Shares held by employees (% *of total shares*)	16.9%	56.6%
Minimum and maximum shares	Min: 1,000 *yuan* Max: 20,000 *yuan*	Min: 10 *yuan* (1 share) Max: 20,000 *yuan* (2,000 shares)
Voting rights	One-share-one-vote	One-member-one-vote
Max shares held (% *of total*)	"Natural person": 0.5% "Legal person": 10%	N.A.
Shares held by top 10 shareholders (% *of total shares*)	34.7%	N.A.

N.A.: not applicable or not available
Source: the rural commercial bank's charter

The problem of insider control has also been attenuated significantly, as indicated by the fall in magnitude of employee-held shares from 56.6 to 16.9 percent. This means that in the previous system, the employees used to have a majority in the member representatives meeting. But, as a group, they now account for less than one-fifth of total shareholders' votes. Further, given the fact that shareholders are more dispersed in the rural cooperative bank than in the rural commercial bank, insider control is more of a problem in the former than in the latter.

Internal Party Committees in the Credit Organizations

The internal party committee is the most pivotal institution within the credit organizations, however it does not exist on paper or charter of the credit cooperative. Yet in the organizations, it is the core decision-making body.[41]

The RCC's Party committee is headed by the Party secretary, who is also the head of the board of directors. He is undoubtedly the top decision maker in the organization (yibashou). The Party committee usually comprises the deputy head of the BOD, who is the second in-charge; the bank governor (hangzhang, in the case of rural commercial banks and rural cooperative banks) or the bank director (zhuren, in the case of rural credit cooperatives); the head of the supervisory board, who is also the Party disciplinary committee member (jilv weiyuanhui); and assistant bank governors, or heads of key departments, such as credit.

It should be noted that some but not all of a bank's typical key executives are Party committee members. The Party committee members are the core decision makers who have major powers over personnel nominations, appointments and dismissals of branch managers. This implies that not every bank executive has substantive and equal power; only those selected into the Party committee are the core decision makers in the organization. While the head of the BOD and bank governor are always in the Party committees, the other key executives, such as head of BOS and assistant bank governors, may or may not be Party committee members.

Interestingly, the executive appointment and appraisal system has an uncanny resemblance to the cadre evaluation system of the Communist Party. The Party committee members themselves—the first-tier personnel—are determined and appraised by the Party committee one level above them. The Party committee of a county union determines that of township RCCs, and the Party committee of a provincial union determines that of county RCCs. Second-tier and ordinary employees in the financial organizations are akin to the ordinary cadres (yiban ganbu) in the Party. Their personnel information, or dossiers, are held by the leadership group or leading cadres (lingdao ganbu) at the same level. Personnel information of the members of the leadership group—akin to leading cadres (lingdao ganbu) in the Party— are evaluated by the Party committee one level immediately above them.[42] The Communist Party's authority on personnel matters includes nominations, appointments, appraisals, reallocations and dismissals of individuals. Aside from personnel decisions, major capital expenditure is also a prerogative of the Party committee. For instance, if a credit cooperative needs to build a new building for one of its fast-growing branches, the decision needs to be studied and approved by the Party committee.[43]

With the exception of those grassroots RCCs that still retain their independent legal entity status, the power of the township Party committees over the post-reform township RCCs has diminished considerably.[44] The post-reform township RCC Party branches are now accountable to the county RCC unions' Party committees. This means that as Party members, they are now evaluated by the county unions' Party committees: township Party committees have no formal control rights over the grassroots RCC officials, though one could argue that informal rights to influence or sway their decisions still exist.[45] Most importantly, since loan decision-making power has been centralized at the county level, the county union's accountability to the local Party committee means that the post-reform credit organization still have to toe the local Party's lines.

In short, the collective action problem of member households and insider control have been attenuated to a greater extent in the post-reform rural commercial bank than in the rural cooperative bank. However, the Party's influence remains forceful in both post-reform credit organizations.

Reconciling Internal Party Institution with the Corporate Governance Structure?

After examining the corporate governance structure and Party institution, a logical question to ask is how could the Party's prerogatives be reconciled with those of the board of directors and members' representative meetings or shareholders' meetings?

The scope and strength of the power of these institutions differ between areas, and the division is by no means clear-cut. On personnel matters, including appointments, promotions and dismissals, the Party committee, irrevocably, has an upper hand. Furthermore, the Party committee also has prerogatives over major financial expenditures, such as employees' remuneration, and building renovation and construction expenditures. Personnel (yongren) and finance (yongqian) are clearly the two areas where the Party committee has power over the formal corporate governance bodies, namely the BOD, or members' representative meeting or shareholders' meeting.[46] As far as loan allocation decisions are concerned, it is far from clear whether the formal corporate governance bodies or Party committees dominate. Party committees in the post-reform credit organizations are not involved in loan allocations. It is impossible to tell whether they were "toeing the official line" or speaking the truth. Nonetheless, it is inconceivable that the coterie that makes a range of decisions from personnel to expenditure can abstain from getting involved in the bank's core business: loan allocations.[47]

A conflict that has arisen in the post-reform corporate governance structure, due to the persistence of Party institutions, is the clashing of the heads of the BOD and the BOS, and the bank governor. In terms of professional functions, as set out in the charter, the head of the BOD is the bank's legal representative and strategic decision maker, while the bank governor, whose power is delegated by the BOD, makes decisions on day-to- day operations, and the head of the BOS plays a supervisory role over the other two. Hence, according to the formal corporate governance rules, there exists a separation of functions between these three positions, and checks and balances against each other's power. Yet, in terms of Party hierarchy or administrative ranking, the head of the BOD, who is also the Party secretary, clearly outranks the other two; and, as Party members, they have to report to the Party secretary. How could a subordinate supervise the Party superior when his performance is in fact evaluated by the superior? By the same token, how could a subordinate prevent the superior from intervening in his work when his failure to follow the superior's instructions will likely result in a dismissal?

The Communist Party and Corporate Governance: What Does it Imply for the Role of Local States in China?

Research studies that examines the nexus between politics and business in China has pointed to the fact that the Communist Party institutions do not compliment well with effective corporate governance structure.[48] Here, we highlight some issues pertinent to the financial institutions.

Matrix Muddle: Functional and Party Accountability

All financial institutions in China, including the rural credit organizations, are subject to two sets of accountability system: the functional/industry and the Communist Party. Figure 5 maps out the accountability system at various administrative levels.

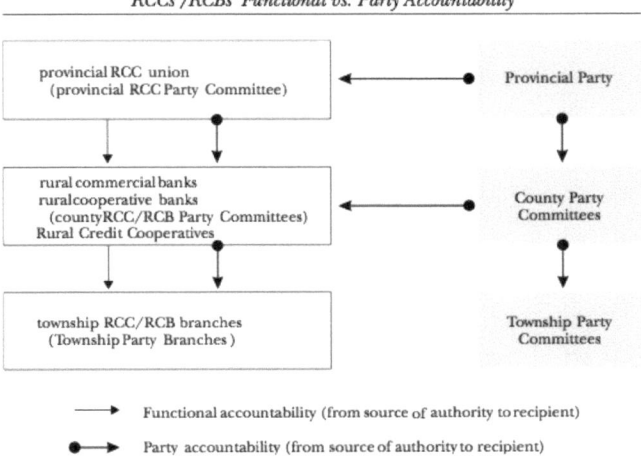

Figure 5
RCCs'/RCBs' Functional vs. Party Accountability

It is highly evident that the two sets of accountability systems are aimed at serving different goals and objectives. On the one hand, the local Party committee has its own interests and priorities, which differ from those of the provincial unions. Based on the Communist Party cadre evaluation system, the local Party committee is evaluated by the Party bosses one level above it. Studies on the Party cadre evaluation criteria show that local economic growth takes priority over other areas of development, such as the environment, education and healthcare.[49] Local economy needs finance to fuel its growth, and the local Party committee uses its political tentacles to pressurize the local financial institutions to extend credit to favored enterprises and projects. Local government interference in credit expansion has been blamed for the bouts of inflation between the late 1980s and early 1990s,[50] and the credit boom in China in the early 2008, despite a slowing down in the global economy.[51]

On the other hand, the interests of the provincial unions, which represent the provincial governments' stake in RCC reform, are not as clear-cut. Several points can be inferred from their operations thus far. Given that a key central government's objective in the reform is to transfer financial responsibility of the loss-making credit institutions to the provincial governments, the provincial unions have an inherent vested interest in the commercial sustainability of the RCCs.[52] This profit orientation is reflected in the professional evaluation criteria, to which RCC officers are subjected, and on which the magnitude of their bonuses depend. The RCC's professional evaluation criteria assess the employees based on an increase in savings, reduction in non-performing loan rates, collection of interest income, profitability and agricultural loan issuance.[53]

If RCC officers are to strictly follow their professional evaluation criteria, they will be allocating loans based on the expected returns of applications. This may not favor local government's enterprises and projects. If profit orientation is the ultimate criterion, RCC officers will favor lending to private enterprises and member households, given the historically high non- performing loan rates of local government-related loans. Hence, it is evident that the Communist Party accountability system is fundamentally incongruent with an effective corporate governance structure and efficient functioning of the financial system.

What does this imply for the role of local states in China? It is taken for granted that fiscal decentralization provides an enormous incentive for the local states to develop industries and promote industrialization. While this behavior is seemingly "entrepreneurial" or "corporatist," it is noteworthy that enterprises need capital financing, and industries require capital investment. Where is the money coming from? This is the question that the existing literature has often failed to ask. When a local government pressures the local credit cooperative to allocate loans to its township-and-village enterprises or industrial projects, the money must be redirected from somewhere else. The loans could have gone to private enterprises and rural households who consistently contribute 80 percent of the RCCs' savings base, and who require credit for a range of production and consumption activities.

Further, the mountains of non-performing loans of the RCCs make it abundantly clear that a majority of the loans to local government-related enterprises and projects have gone sour. In short, when the costs of local industrialization are fully taken into consideration, the role of local states is far from "developmental," as the existing literature has depicted.

Section 5: Other Goals of the Chinese Government

These lending trends in themselves should be sufficient to raise concerns about the quality of bank loan portfolios and the need to curtail growth of bank lending in coming years, but there is additionally the Chinese central administration's own declared intention to move away from "excessive" reliance on investment as the engine of growth. An increased share of GDP going to consumption reduces demand for bank loans and drains the household savings currently held as bank deposits. This is in line with the government's objective of allowing the relative importance of banks to decrease in coming years while promoting the profile of securities markets.

China's membership in the WTO in December 2001 has also ushered in a new era for Chinese banks. China committed to full opening of its banking sector to foreign competition after a five-year transition period, although to this day e.g. the insurance sector and securities markets are still not completely open to foreign participants. The threat of tougher competition meant that banks, especially state-owned banks, had to become more efficient in their operations. This called for changes in the governance and ownership structures of banks, and more importantly, bank balance sheets had to be strengthened. Simply put, the government had to deal with the NPL issue decisively.

Section 6: The Other Commonly Forgotten Goal – Increasing the Relevance of the Rural Banking Sector

For the overall banking sector in China, total after-tax profit reached RMB 899.1 billion in 2010, a one-third increase from 2009. The increased profit contributed to higher profitability ratios. Return on equity (ROE) went up by more than 1% to 17.5%; return on assets (ROA) was 1%. Large commercial banks accounted for about 57% of total banking sector profits, well above their share of total banking sector assets (49%). Their share in banking sector profits has not changed significantly in recent years.

However, here comes the disparity: Rural credit cooperatives only accounted for a miserly 2.6% of banking sector profits, while their share of sector assets was almost 7%.

For a banking sector that serves three-quarters of the country's population in the rural areas, having such a minor share of banking sector profits and total sector assets proves to undermine the relevance of the rural banking sector in China.

It is at this stage that we believe that the development of the urban-related banking sector has been given far more attention and resources as compared to that of the rural banking sector, and that increasing the overall market relevance of the rural counterparts has often been a forgotten, or least-emphasized aim within the industry.

In the following section, we provide solutions that can increase the relevance of the rural commercial banks in the near future. Such increase in relevance will bode well for the development of the entire commercial banking sector, allowing them to diversify away from, and rely less on the major commercial banks to spearhead growth.

Section 7: Rural Banking Sector Reforms for a Brighter Future

The livelihood of the millions living in the rural areas of China for the next few generations to come are now contingent on how the future of rural commercial banking in China will evolve. Here, the authors will highlight the policies that will be beneficial through the achievement of 4 main goals:

1. Effective Resource Allocation
2. The reduction of the Principal-Agent Problem
3. The reduction of the Collective Action Problem
4. The reduction of the incongruence between the Communist Party accountability system with the corporate governance structure of an efficiently functioning rural commercial banking system

It is through these objectives that the future of rural banking in China must aim at for the betterment of the rural community that it is meant to serve.

It is at this juncture that the authors also realized that in order to meet these meaningful objectives, active efforts in reforms have to be made in entities and best practices that go way beyond the rural banking industry. The rural banking industrial relies on an ecosystem that comprises a broader group of stakeholders (e.g. party officials at different levels, bank employees who are also shareholders...), shared mechanisms (e.g. decision making mechanisms, check-and-balance mechanisms) and even pricing mechanisms (e.g. for loans and other products). Facets of these elements that form the larger ecosystem of rural banking in China will be brought up in our proposed solutions.

Effective Resource Allocation

Effective resource allocation, in the context of China's rural banking system, can be sub-divided into 2 frameworks.

The first involves the effective allocation of loans and the interest charged on these loans, and the subsequent reduction of non-performing loans (NPLs).

The second involves the creation of new and novel bank products that best serves the unique needs of market segments within the rural consumers and business community.

In other words, resource allocative efficiency means that the correct funds (and type of funds) have to go to the correct borrower, at the correct rate, and at the correct timeframe.

Rural Banks to Go Public

Perhaps the most major and most explicit transformation of rural banks in the future that we both anticipate, and recommend, is that rural banks will seek to get listed in main boards or small-chip boards. This is currently divergent from the business structure of most rural banks, where only the bigger and more established banks such as the Bank of Chongqing are listed.

Being listed will force banks to be more efficient, to increase their corporate governance standards, move towards a more liberalized public disclosure regime, and ultimately, create heightened relevance within the financial system due to increased market integration.

It is only through such a shift that market efficiency in this sector can rapidly increase her efficiency, at least through the reduction of asymmetric information from the beginning stages.

Because a wider group of shareholders are now involved, banks are further encouraged to improve their loan decision-making process and reduce any incidents on having NPLs simply due to political pressure at the provincial level.

For example, if the amount of NPLs were to shoot up in a particular quarter, and sustain itself throughout the entire financial year, bank balance sheets that report these will decrease investors' confidence in the share itself, resulting in a decline in share price for the bank in question.

Therefore, through public disclosure in both the primary and secondary market proceedings, going public essentially serves up as an additional check-and-balance system that these banks will need to ensure the vitality of the loan-granting system, the very core business they are in.

This effect will be all the more prominent, given that employees of these banks traditionally, and collectively hold shares of up to 25% in the banks they serve (See Table 1 and Table 2 in the section on *Issues in Rural Banking – Unsolved and New, Emerging Issues from the Post-Reform Era*). Because personal stake and personal share ownership is involved, bank employees will be encouraged to see themselves as "business owners" of the bank, rather than just employees following the orders of their superiors.

Even better the result be, if enlightened leadership from the relevant party committees will take the long term share prices of these rural banks as an indicator of performance, rather than whether the decision making authority within these banks have supported TVEs through loans granted.

A complimentary mechanism that our group will propose is the Dual-Financing System. It is this very system that will remove any potential conflict of interest the Provincial Governments will have in terms of their loan-seeking behavior to fund their TVEs, with the bank management's inherent desire to reduce NPLs. The Dual-Financing System will be further expounded on in Part 4 of this Section.

Also, it is evident that by securitizing the bank and her assets through IPO, and subsequently by enhancing its liquidity through the trading of these shares through a secondary market, the government's goal of developing the equity market will definitely be met through this initiative. The equity market currently stands at a small percentage of the entire banking sector.

This can be done in tandem that State-owned banks continue serving as both a policy tool, and an economic development tool.

Further, more benefits will be achieved just by going public.

Firstly, this is in line with the government's objective of reducing the urban-rural divide. By going public, rural banks will be forced to be more efficient and decrease any chances of NPLs, thereby allowing for more loans and credit to be available to the private sector within these rural areas. More available credit means decrease interest rates and lower cost of funds for these private rural enterprises. This will in turn stimulate rural and agricultural development within the rural areas, increasing the income of the rural community and reducing the Gini Coefficient that shows the difference in income and wealth the urban rich has as compared to the rural poor.

Second, banks will be forced to improve on their efficiency and business functions, and to start seeing themselves more as independent enterprises, rather than just another extension of the Communist Party.

Third, it will also increase the quality and efficiency of government projects. Government officials wanting to raise funds/loans for their pet projects through a publicly listed commercial bank, will have to ensure that the quality of their projects meet certain reasonable requirements, for example, through cash flow projections like the DCF (Discounted Cash Flow) or WACC requirements (Weighted Average Cost of Capital). These projects' credit history will also be scrutinized.

It therefore becomes a mechanism that encourages government officials to increase the quality of their projects, and that only projects confident enough in meeting the requirements for loans will be put forward to these banks, creating a self-selection environment.

Forth, the equity markets will thus become more vibrant and robust, allowing investors a wider selection of stocks to select from, just from the banking sector alone. This will draw a wider range of investors with different investment preferences and risk profiles to the equities market, enhancing the overall liquidity of the entire trading environment.

Even better that this will "domesticate" the local investment environment. Instead of having local portfolio managers from local investment institutions choosing to allocate their portfolio into e.g. the Hang Seng Index, due to the vibrant listings of banking institutions on that board, these portfolio managers can now have an alternative platform to invest, and can therefore allocate their funds domestically (versus having fund outflows into Hong Kong shares).

Fifth, shareholders will benefit immensely. Take for example the farmer who owns the shares of the local rural bank will have the incentive to utilize government grants and subsidies on top of loans, and work hard so as to repay these loans to the bank, allowing for a decreased in NPLs.

The farmer's gain is therefore threefold:

1. Increased productivity.
2. Increased value of his shares via the local bank, assuming if other farmers who own shares of the local bank were to behave in the same way, ceteris paribus.
3. Enhanced credit history of the individual, which will allow him to gain more loans at lower cost to fuel future business expansions.

Larger loans garnered in subsequent business development stages by rural companies will in turn, encourage large-scale and regional commercial banks to dedicate more funds to rural development, and to increase the loans they are willing to dedicate towards rural private entities.

Sixth, through the above benefits, with a stronger and more robust financial system that made up of individual banks which has lesser incidents of non-performing loans, better corporate governance, increased relevance within the financial system, enhanced profitability and efficiency, the government, who has had policies conservative in nature in the past, will then be in a better position to allow foreign banks to enter the rural banking industry, in line with her 2001 WTO Ascension pack. This will mean a more robust financial industrial to support rural development.

Foster the Creation of a Wider Variety of Government Schemes

In addition encouraging these rural commercial banks to go public, the government will do well to foster the development of more government grants, subsidies and incentives for rural agricultural and industrial enterprises.

For example, a newly created government platform that supports rural agricultural and industrial entrepreneurs will have the following benefits:

1. A network of advisers and entrepreneurs willing to share contacts and share advise with these entrepreneurs.
2. Additional sources of funding. Where bank loans and private, informal loans are the main means that these entrepreneurs have to rely on in the past for their fund raising efforts, they can now look forward to government grants (e.g. the government can match a dollar to every dollar that the entrepreneur raised). And if the entrepreneur achieves multiple milestones, the government can then further reward them with additional funds, through the Milestone Funding Concept.
3. The application of these funds can also serve as a valuable Feedback Mechanism that these entrepreneurs need. For example, an entrepreneur wanting to apply for these government grants will need to submit an application to the local provincial office etc. Whether he succeeds or fails in getting the grant, he will still receive valuable feedback on the areas he needs to improve, and on the parts of his business plan that is already done well. Such fundamental feedbacks, given by a panel of judges that comprises of successful entrepreneurs, academics etc, will allow these rural businesses valuable suggestions to fundamentally improve their businesses from ground up.
4. Successful businesses that went through this scheme can then approach banks in subsequent stages of their business funding process, and will have better chances of negotiating for more affordable loans, because they have already been *pre-selected* by government grant-awarding bodies.

Foster the Creation of a Wider Variety of Financial Products

Similarly, we recommend that rural banks create a wider variety of financial products to serve the diverse needs of her rural clients. These financial products can be further classified into two types:

1. Savings and Financing Products, such as the creation of a land mortgage system
2. Risk Mitigation and Risk Transfer Products, such as insurance schemes

Farmers in rural areas might be asset rich, but unfortunately, cash poor. Despite having assessed amounts of land, the farmer or farming family, in the perspective of an agricultural entrepreneur, will require capital to buy equipment, funds as salaries to hire more people to work the land etc.

Unfortunately, these hardworking people lived in a market that cannot value well the land that these farmers possess. In other words, there are high price-discovery costs in terms of wanting to accurately discover the exact valuation of their land, and high transaction costs in wanting to sell or rent this land to raise capital for business expenditure and expansion.

Adding to their woes is that private ownership of these lands might not have the backing of a fully effective legal system. This can be seen that land ownership and land boundaries are often heavily contested within rural communities, and remain ambiguous in title deeds. This therefore makes land valuation all the more difficult.

However, having a land mortgage system is one of the few other ways that provides these farmers an additional avenue in fund raising. These excess lands can serve well as a collateral to garner loans. Banks that offers such loan will in effect, also need to create a mechanism to value effectively these real estates, thereby creating a positive externality in the form of increasing the rural market's knowledge capital in terms of land and real estate valuation.

Apart from the creation of savings and financing products, insurance products are also needed in the industry to transfer and mitigate both personal and business risks. Currently, the rural community is most underserved by insurance products.

This is because of the following reasons:

1. Rural businesses and her accompanying risks are difficult to value and ascertain, for example, those risks in the operational risk category, thus placing additional informational search costs that deter major insurance companies from creating suites of comprehensive insurance packages specifically targeting only the rural poor.
2. Distribution channels are fragmented in rural communities, making it costly to create a single insurance policy that can be effectively distributed and marketed to different rural areas spread throughout the country.
3. Consumer buying behavior: For business owners from the developing regions in rural areas, business and general insurances aren't the first thing that comes to mind when starting out, as immediate business expenditures take precedence.

These problems can be solved in two ways:

1. If the government were to set up a formal grant-making body as we have described above, they can include the insurance schemes as part of the overall value of the business grant or subsidies that they offer.
2. Through the creation of various loan schemes and financial products, such as the land mortgage financing scheme mentioned above, these rural banks can then offer these much-needed insurance schemes as part of the value of the overall loans they offer, or that businessmen getting these loans will have the option to opt into one of these insurance schemes at a subsidized or affordable rate.

These insurance schemes are much needed in rural areas, to guard against losses from e.g. natural disasters on crop harvest, and damaged goods caused by accidents on poorly maintained roads in rural areas during transportation. The mitigation of such losses through insurance will encourage the rural entrepreneur to raise funds through formal means, like loans from banks, thereby increasing the relevance of rural commercial banks towards the very market segment it is supposed to serve.

Encourage Foreign Bank Participation

It is evident that the inclusion of foreign players in the banking industry will spur greater competition, better innovation and enhanced efficiency between both local banks and foreign banks alike. Despite the increased competition that will unsettle especially the smaller local banks, these banks can create avenues to collaborate with foreign banks in terms of financial product development, co-branding of financial products, or even through the co-sharing of bank facilities such as ATM machines, thus increasing the robustness in terms of product and service offerings, and potentially decrease costs.

Further, the inclusion of foreign banks into the rural industry is only a matter of time, given China's ascension to the WTO in 2001.

To encourage more foreign bank participation in rural banking in China in the long run, we recommend that regulations be altered to

1. Reduce the capital requirements needed by these banks to set up branches
2. Reduce capital adequacy ratio (CAR) or increase loans-deposits ratio to encourage foreign bank's lending to rural development. This will increase the money supply and reduce the cost of loans to the development of small, rural businesses

The reduction of the cost of loans through increased money supply will encourage entrepreneurs and businesses to seek bank loans over private loans from family/friends (informal fundraising means) etc. Informal fundraising means as described is currently the most major substitute to formal fundraising means like bank loans.

Unfortunately, there are now relatively high capital requirements for bank branches in comparison to domestic banks to encourage foreign banks to incorporate locally (Herd et al., 2010). KPMG (2010) notes that locally incorporated foreign banks face a deadline in 2011 to reduce their loan-to-deposit ratios to 75 %.

In addition, there are still restrictions on foreign investors in commercial banks. For example, the maximum foreign share for an individual investor in commercial banks is 20%, and the total foreign investment allowed is at most 25%. Such restrictions have to be removed, or at least, lightened, in order to encourage foreign participation in China's rural banking industry.

It should also be noted that many of the banks where the state holds a majority stake also have foreign owners. From the Chinese side, foreign banks' strategic ownership has been hoped to provide improvements in corporate governance and technical efficiency. Foreign shareholders, in turn, are seeking easier access to the Chinese banking market.

Development of a Strong Interbank Market

By and large, Chinese banks are involved in traditional banking services. This is reflected in the structure of their balance sheets. On the funding side, deposits from enterprises and households are the single most important liability class.

At the end of 2004, deposits still constituted 72.6% of total liabilities.

However, at the end of 2009, 68.3% of commercial bank liabilities were deposits from non-financial institutions and households; total liabilities to non-financial institutions and households were 70.0% (People's Bank of China, 2010).

This therefore shows that in recent years, bank funding has begun to shift away from deposits.

As the importance of deposits from the public has decreased, the role of other financial institutions has increased. It appears that interbank markets have become more important as a source of funds, especially for smaller banks and other financial institutions that benefit from funds provided by larger banks.

At the end of 2009, 5.6% of bank liabilities were to other financial institutions. Compare this to the figures we obtained at the end of 2004, where the corresponding share was only 2.0%.

While this phenomenal highlighted above are representative for commercial banks in general, we foresee and recommend that a strong interbank market that involves the rural banking community be created.

The benefits are multiple.

First, the creation of an effective interbank market for rural banks will allow for a diversification of sources of funds and sources of liabilities for Rural Commercial Banks. No longer do these banks have to rely on deposits from the rural communities as a main source of funds. Rural private enterprises and individuals collectively provides for a massive 80% of the total funds to rural commercial banks, in terms of deposits.

Second, the development of the interbank market is much needed to provide cheap funding sources for local rural banks. This will in turn allow for cheaper loans and enhanced credit assess to rural areas, reducing the cost of loans that rural entrepreneurs will have to bear with.

Finally, smaller banks will benefit from funds provided by larger banks and foreign banks that have operations in urban areas. Such will encourage capital flows from the urban areas to the rural areas, to the benefit of rural development.

Allow Rural Banks more leeway in setting their own interest rates

We will encourage that rural commercial banks be allowed more leeway to set their own interest rates for deposits and loans. This can be done by increasing the interest rate band that banks can operate with vis-à-vis the benchmark rate set by the central commercial bank. This will be an important effect of decentralization and liberalization, and will force banks to be more efficient and to adopt more efficient loan pricing models.

Banks benefit from the large spread between loan and deposit rates still determined by the central bank. Prior to 2004, lending rates of commercial banks were allowed to deviate from the benchmark rate set by the central bank by no more than 10%.

After 2004, the bands were widened and currently commercial banks have a bit more freedom in setting rates as commercial bank lending rates are only subject to a floor and deposits rates to a ceiling (OECD, 2010). The bank loan interest rate margins measured by the spread between the weighted average interest rate on bank loans and the benchmark interest rate have been decreasing over time.

Allow Rural Banks to play a more major financing role in Developmental Projects

We foresee that in the future, the next development pathway that rural commercial banks can adopt is the creation of private equity arms as part of their investment strategy.

These private equity arms will be equipped to buy into stakes of rural developmental projects from the private sector that shows promising potential future growth.

The benefits to rural development projects are numerous. In the past when banks only provide loans to rural enterprises, they do not have the incentive to monitor and support the growth of these projects. But now, with rural private enterprises needing financing at the same time, these rural commercial banks, in holding an equity stake in these rural private enterprises, will be more incentivize to provide the relevant support needed for the success of these projects. These much needed support can range from corporate governance advisory, connections to business opportunities, or even future funding possibilities.

Also by owning an equity stake do these banks be able to achieve representation in shareholder meetings and board of directors meetings, allowing these banks to monitor and play an active role in guiding promising rural enterprises.

For these banks, another major benefit will be from the diversification of income sources. Okazaki et al. (2011) estimate that net interest income accounted for 82% of the operating profit in the major listed commercial banks and another important source was net fee-based income (13%). The authors attribute this to the increase of loans.

However, by operating a strong private equity arm, banks can diversify from the traditional net interest income and net fee-based income, and increase their overall investment income instead. This diversification will diversify the operational risks of banks, yet still allow banks to ride on the wave of high savings rate in the country.

Develop the Equity and Bond Markets as Alternative Sources of Financing

By encourage rural commercial banks to issue shares (as mentioned in the point above), the rural equity markets can then be better developed.

Banks should also seek to issue bonds and other fixed income financing products. Not only will this increase the overall market vibrancy due to the increase in the universe of financial products made available to the rural man on the street, but it will also provide rural households an added avenue for investments and risk diversification, on top of the traditional savings deposit that they used to rely on.

Dual-Financing Scheme

From the readings above, our report has highlighted that the Communist Party accountability system is fundamentally incongruent with an effective corporate governance structure and efficient functioning of the financial system.

If RCC officers are to strictly follow their professional evaluation criteria, they will be allocating loans based on the expected returns of applications. This may not favor local government's enterprises and projects.

If profit orientation is the ultimate criterion, RCC officers will favor lending to private enterprises and member households, given the historically high non-performing loan rates of local government-related loans.

At this stage, in order to solve this incongruence, our group actually proposes the development of what we call, the Dual-Funding System. This system entails that township and village enterprises (TVEs) under the purview of local party officials can only get funding from the Central Government funding sources, and are not supposed to get funded via the rural commercial banks.

These rural commercial banks will therefore only serve the funding needs of those private enterprises.

Although we recognize that such a system will depart massively from the current rural banking system, in which TVEs are allowed to garner funds and loans from rural commercial banks and credit cooperatives, such a system that distinguish the funding sources available for the two enterprises (TVEs versus public) has numerous advantages.

Firstly, it solves immediately the problem of the incongruence between corporate governance goals and the communist party's accountability system. Through such a separation of funding sources, this conflict of interest in the granting of loans will immediately cease to exist.

Second, for TVEs to get loans from the Central Government's funding sources, they will need to ensure the viability and feasibility of their projects before approaching the Central Government for funds. This self-selection mechanism (which is a positive externality granted through this new funding system) will ensure that

1. Provincial and local governors will have to work harder and do a more thorough thought analysis in order to be confident enough to submit their proposal, all the more knowing that their proposal will be scrutinized by their superiors and which might affect their promotions,
2. And that only the peaches (the good quality projects) will be put forward for funding, while the lemons (the poorer quality projects), will be weeded out. See The Lemon Principle for more details.

This immediately increases the quality of government-related projects by TVEs put forward for funding, improving rural economic development at its core!

In the long run, given that better quality projects will be put forward, the standards of these government projects will be forced to increase, given a pool of limited government funding available at any period of time. In effect, the peaches have crowded out the lemons.

Finally, another important benefit is that funds and deposits raised from the private sector, can, and should, finally go back to serving the fundraising needs of the private sector. No longer will they face the problem of having a lack of credits available to fund private enterprises, despite having 80% of the deposits coming form the private sector.

Develop a Competency-Based Human Resource Development Plan

In this report, we have also highlighted that rarely any new blood is injected into the top management sector after reforms. This reflects that there is a lack of qualified banking personnel in the localities.

To solve this problem, our group proposes the development of a competency-based human resource development plan. This plan is crucial to increase the talent inflows needed in order to implement and oversee the critical transitions the rural banking industry is facing right now.

Typical features that make up such a system can include:

1. Setting up a platform of advisors that has commercial banking experience
2. Setting up a system that selects and nurtures leaders and talent organically
3. Conduct joint collaborations with partner firms within the rural banking industry so as to foster greater knowledge sharing and interbank hiring
4. Create formal training and development programs, or certification programs, that are useful and relevant in equipping bank practitioners with the relevant skills needed for the role
5. Foster collaborations with local universities to create university programs and continuing education programs (CEPs) relevant to the changing needs of the rural banking industry
6. Create scholarships and research grants that will serve to increase the knowledge capital and prestige of the industry

We recommend that a task force be form to oversee the setting up and implementation of this program. The task force can include senior local party officials, senior rural bank executives, and external advisors with commercial banking experience (e.g. academics, retired executives). The reasons for such a coordinated board is to ensure that a diverse set of views are heard and are well represented, needs are met and creativity maximized, thereby reducing any incidence of groupthink.

Section 8: Conclusion

The collective action problem and insider control problem are some of the major themes in this report, propelling our group to set out in recommending a set of relevant, practical policy changes that we hope will characterize the future of rural banking in China. It is with this very goal – the goal of an efficiently functioning rural banking system that will support and improve the livelihood of the millions dependent on these services in generations to come – that motivates us to do as thorough a research that we can to address these fundamental issues.

With regards to the collective action problem that still exists, we can simply recommend that an increasingly stringent cap on the maximum number of shareholders be allowed in any rural cooperative bank. In other words, the number of shareholders have to decrease from the current 13,500 due to this stringent cap, ensuring that the shares are less thinly spread.

We can also simply pass a regulation that increases the maximum share ownership of any single shareholder. Currently, a corporation and its related companies or the "legal person" can only hold a maximum of 0.5 percent of total shares, while bank employees and other "natural persons" can hold 1.5 and 0.5 percent, respectively.

However, while on the surface, a layman policy practitioner will believe that the policy recommendations highlighted in the preceding two paragraphs will effectively reduce the collective action problem as shareholders will have a greater stake in the rural commercial bank, and are therefore incentivized to monitor the bank closely, our group feels that the implementation of such policies do not solve the root of the problem. Not even the slightest bit.

By going public, a recommendation that our group expounded on in the preceding section, only then will such a problem of collective monitoring be effectively solved.

Going public allows for greater transparency, and through a full and fair disclosure regime, allow for more effective monitoring to take place.

Through the trading of these shares in the secondary market, market forces will be more heavily involved in the valuation of these rural commercial banks, allowing for investors that truly believe in the fair value of these banks to acquire more shares of these banks. These are the group of shareholders that will have the inventive to monitor the activities of these banks.

Therefore, it is only through such a radical change that the collective action problem be eliminated.

On top of solving this problem, and with effective government aid, we sincerely believe that the suggested recommendations are useful in creating a more robust rural banking industry. Coupled this with the inclusion of foreign competitors years ahead (to happen when the local commercial banks are at least ready for such competition), the rural banking industry will be more vibrant than ever before, with these foreign banks forcing the increase in standard, innovation and efficiency of local bank operations.

It is only by then that such a virtuous cycle will take place, where development breeds development, and positive externalities impacting rural private enterprises and households, such as the variations of bank products available, and through lower costs of credit, will ensue.

References and Notes

1   Nicholas Lardy, China's Unfinished Economic Revolution (Washington, DC: Brookings Institution Press, 1998).

2   Sebastian Heilmann, "Policy-making and Political Supervision in Shanghai's Financial Industry," Journal of Contemporary China, vol. 14, no. 45 (2005), pp. 643-668.

3   Victor Shih, Factions and Finance in China: Elite Conflict and Inflation (Cambridge, New York: Cambridge University Press, 2008).

4   See Christopher A. McNally, "Strange Bedfellows: Communist Party Institutions and New Governance Mechanisms in Chinese State Holding Corporations," Business and Politics, vol. 4, no. 1 (2002), pp. 91-115.

5   For instance, see Susan Whiting, Power and Wealth in Rural China: The Political Economy of Institutional Change (New York: Cambridge University Press, 2001); Maria Edin, "Remaking the Communist Party-State: The Cadre Responsibility System at the Local Level in China," China: An International Journal, vol. 1, no. 1 (2003), pp. 1-15; John P. Burns, "Strengthening Central CCP Control of Leadership Selection: The 1990s Nomenklatura," The China Quarterly, vol. 138 (1994), pp. 458-491.

6   Zhongguo jinrong xuehui, Almanac of China's Finance and Banking [Zhongguo jinrong nianjian] (Beijing: Almanac of China's Finance and Banking Editor Board, various years).

7   Loren Brandt, Albert Park and Sangui Wang, "Are China Financial Reforms Leaving the Poor Behind?," in Yasheng Huang, T. Saich and E. Steinfeld, eds.,

Financial Sector Reform in China (Cambridge, Massachusetts: Harvard University Asia Center, 2005).

8   Michael Jensen and William Meckling, "Theory of the Firm: Managerial Behavior, Agency Costs, and Ownership Structure," Journal of Financial Economics, vol. 3 (1976), pp. 305-360.

9   Lynette Ong, "Multiple Principals and Collective Action: China's Rural Credit Cooperatives and Poor Households' Access to Credit," Journal of East Asian Studies, vol. 6, no. 2 (2006), pp. 177-204.

10   Jean C. Oi, Rural China Takes Off (Berkeley: University of California Press, 1999); Lynette Ong, "The Political Economy of Credit in Rural China: The Rural Credit Cooperatives," Australian National University, Ph.D. thesis; Whiting, Power and Wealth in Rural China: The Political Economy of Institutional Change.

11   Oi, Rural China Takes Off ; Jean C. Oi, "Fiscal Reform and the Economic Foundations of Local State Corporatism in China," World Politics, vol. 45, no. 1 (1992), pp. 99-126.

12   Jane Duckett, The Entrepreneurial State in China: Real Estate and Commerce Departments in Reform- era Tianjin (London and New York: Routledge, 1998).

13   Marc Blecher and Vivienne Shue, Tethered Deer: Government and Economy in a Chinese County (Stanford, California: Stanford University Press, 1996).

14   In some parts of rural China where private enterprises are vibrant, such as Wenzhou prefecture in Zhejiang province, informal finance plays a greater role in supplying rural residents with much-needed capital financing. For further information, see Kellee S. Tsai, Back-Alley Banking: Private Entrepreneurs in China (Ithaca, New York: Cornell University Press, 2002).

15   Xiaochuan Zhou, "The Central Bank's Role in the Rural Credit Cooperatives' Reforms" [Zhongyang yinhang zai Nongxinshe gaige zhong de jueshe], 21 Century Economic Report [21 shiji jingji baoda], 23 August 2004.

16   From the author's field interviews with retired RCC officers.

17   The county credit unions in turn had to report to the central bank's offices at the local level.

18   Ping Xie, "Debates on the Reforms of China's Rural Credit Cooperatives' System" [Zhongguo Nongcun Xingyonghezoushe Tizhi Gaige de Zhenglun], Jinrong Yanjiu [Journal of Financial Research], vol. 1 (2001), pp. 1-13.

19   Ning Yu, "An Investigation of the Repayment Situations of the Central Bank's On-lending" [Yanghang zaidaikuan changhuan qingkuang diaocha], Finance and Economics [Caijin], (5 August 2003).

20   During the years of high inflation, in order to guarantee positive savings rates to the savers, some of the RCCs were forced to pay out such high savings rates that it ate into their profitability.

21   Lynette Ong, "The Political Economy of Township Government Debt, Township Enterprises and Rural Financial Institutions in China," The China Quarterly, vol. 186 (2006), pp. 377-400.

22   In Chinese language, they are known as "zhuangxiang zhongyang yinhang piaoju" (earmarked central bank bill) and "zhuangxiang zhongyang yinhang daikuan" (earmarked central bank loans). All the provinces undergoing reforms have chosen to have the earmarked central bank bills, with the exception of Jilin and Shaanxi, that opted for the earmarked central bank lending. Those poor-performing RCCs that have an excess of liabilities over assets (zibudizhai) based on their

financial figures in 2002 year-end were qualified to apply for the earmarked central bank's bills or earmarked central bank's lending. The excess is calculated based on a formula taking into account the value of non-performing loans, and liability-offsetting assets (dizhaizhichan). Sources: China Banking Regulatory Authority, "Operation of the Central Bank's Earmarked Bills for the RCCs in Pilot Reform Areas," Document No. 181 (3 September 2003), China Banking Regulatory Authority, "Management of the Rural Credit Cooperatives' Earmarked Lending in Pilot Reform Areas" [Nongcun xinyongshe gaige shidian zhuanxiang jiekuan guanli banfa]. Document No. 181 (3 September 2003). The bonds pay an annual interest rate of 1.89 percent, and cashing-out of the bonds are conditional upon the RCCs meeting requirements on capital adequacy ratios, and certain nominal changes in corporate governance structure. Further, the earmarked Central Bank's loans came with a low annual interest rate of 0.945 percent.

23   Lynette Ong, "Local Government Debt: Another Bail-Out Job," China Economic Quarterly, vol. 1 (2006), pp. 48-52.

24   That said, there has been little evidence that the provincial governments have matched the central government's contribution. According to some rural finance specialists in China, local government's matching is spotty; rich provinces typically contribute more than poorer ones do.

25   For a historical account of the various phases of RCC development, see Andrew Watson, "Financing Farmers: The Reform of Rural Credit Cooperatives and Provision of Financial Services to Farmers," in Christopher Findlay, Andrew Watson, Enjiang Cheng and Gang Zhu, eds., Rural Financial Markets in China (Canberra: Asia-Pacific Press, 2003).

26   Watson, "Financing Farmers."

27   The co-existence of the board of directors and board of supervisors is unique to China. The idea of a supervisory board is borrowed from Germany. Cooperatives in other countries may not have a supervisory board. However, the central idea of the corporate governance of cooperative organizations remains the same—the members' representative meeting is the highest decision-making body where nominations and decisions for the people who sit on the board of directors are made.

28   From Ong, "The Political Economy of Credit in Rural China: The Rural Credit Cooperatives," pp. 105-138.

29   From interviews with a number of members of BODs, including independent directors from rural commercial banks.

30   In the case of a rural cooperative bank in Zhejiang, the loan approval committee, made up of the bank governor, assistant governor, chief accountant, and several department heads, has the right to make decisions on any loan to an individual borrower exceeding five million yuan, or any loan to an enterprise borrower exceeding 10 million yuan. Any loans exceeding those amounts have to be submitted for consideration to a risk management committee (fengxian guanli weiyuanhui), a committee under the BOD. While the committee does not approve loans, it assesses the risk profiles of the borrowers and the projects, and subsequently passes the information to the BOD for decision making. The BOD makes decisions on a simple-majority vote based on the total number of board members.

31   Further, there are eight departments operating under the bank governor office: security, audit, technology, finance and accounts, business expansion, human resources and general administration. All departments report directly to the bank governor office. This information was obtained during the author's conversations with high-ranking banking officers during dinner or other informal events.

32   This information was obtained during the author's conversations with high-ranking banking officers during dinner or other informal events.

33   If it is a major crime, the committee hands the individual over to the police. Source: the author's interviews with a few party committee members in credit cooperatives and banks.

34   The senior management of the rural commercial banks has been able to tell me what the heads of the BOS have done, such as monitor whether the BOD decisions abide by the banks' charters. Most of the rural cooperative bank and RCC managers openly admit that the BOS exists only in nominal terms.

35   The Shanghai City Commercial Bank was previously the Shanghai Urban Credit Cooperatives. When the commercial bank was first established, the top management consisted of the same people as those in the urban credit cooperatives. However, there was a gradual replacement in top management by recruiting qualified banking professionals from the industry as the bank grows over time. Source: Author's interview with a senior officer from the Shanghai City Commercial Bank.

36   See Ong, "Multiple Principals and Collective Action: China's Rural Credit Cooperatives and Poor Households' Access to Credit," pp. 177-204.

37   The internal document was made available.

38   All comparisons in this paper are done using one example from each institutional model because little difference was discovered in rural cooperative banks or rural credit cooperatives between different provinces. And in the case of rural commercial banks, there were only a handful in southern Jiangsu, the institutional designs of which hardly differ.

39   The "eligibility threshold" that is equivalent to one vote is 1,000 shares for a "natural person" and 10,000 shares for a "legal person."

40   From an interview with a retired official from a provincial office of the People's Bank of China. This was later confirmed by an interview with an economics professor who has been an advisor to the provincial government on RCC reforms.

41   This conclusion is drawn from previous work on the RCCs. The supreme power of the Party committee is also confirmed in scholarly work on state holding companies and other financial institutions in China, such as McNally, "Strange Bedfellows: Communist Party Institutions and New Governance Mechanisms in Chinese State Holding Corporations"; Heilmann, "Regulatory Innovation by Leninist Means: Communist Party Supervision in China's Financial Industry," pp. 1-21.

42   For instance, see Hon S. Chan, "Cadre Personnel Management in China: The Nomenklatura System, 1990-1998," The China Quarterly, vol. 179, (2004), pp. 703-734; Edin, "Remaking the Communist Party-State: The Cadre Responsibility System at the Local Level in China"; John P. Burns, ""Downsizing" the Chinese State: Government Retrenchment in the 1990s," The China Quarterly, vol. 175 (2003), pp. 775-802.

43   From interviews with a few Party committee members, and high-ranking rural bank officers.

44   Previously, each township RCC had a Party committee (dangwei): a Party unit containing a Party secretary leading a group of Party members. On the contrary, after the reforms, each township RCC only has a Party branch (dangzhibu), which is nothing more than a constellation of Party members (more than three), that has no decision-making power over major Party issues, such as utilization of funds or personnel appointments, management or dismissals. Local (township) Party committees should not be confused with Party committees in township RCCs. The

former is the Party organization at the township administrative level, to which all Party units in local enterprises and units report; and the latter is the Party organization in the credit organization.

45 From an interview with a township RCC manager.

46 This has been repeatedly confirmed by a dozen interviews with Party committee members and banking professionals.

47 Interestingly, the provincial union in Zhejiang has formally reaffirmed the status of the Party committee as the supreme decision-making body in these credit organizations. The Zhejiang provincial union has issued a document instructing (zhishi) all rural credit cooperatives and rural cooperative banks in the province that all major decisions have to be studied (yanjiu) by the Party committees before they are broached for discussions at the shareholders' meetings or board meetings. See Fangyi Zhu, "Identify the Circumstances, Strengthen Leadership, Improve Implementations, Ensure Annual Work Objectives are Realized: Zhu Fangyi's Speech at the Inaugural Members' Representative Meeting at the Provincial Rural Credit Union" (2005).

48 On the corporate governance of state holding companies, see McNally, "Strange Bedfellows"; on the financial sector reform in Shanghai, see Heilmann, "Policy-making and Political Supervision in Shanghai's Financial Industry," pp. 643-668.

49 For instance, see Elizabeth Economy, The Rivers Runs Black: The Environmental Challenge to China's Future (Ithaca, NY: Cornell University Press, 2004); Whiting, Power and Wealth in Rural China: The Political Economy of Institutional Change.

50 Yasheng Huang, Inflation and Investment Controls in China: The Political Economy of Central-Local Relations During the Reform Era (Cambridge: Cambridge

University Press, 1996).

51   Victor Shih, "China's Credit Boom," Wall Street Journal, 21 February 2008.

52   Ping Xie, Xu Zhong and Minggao Shen, "RCC Reforms: What Have We Done? What Do We Still Need to Do?," (2006). Since the provincial governments have taken over financial responsibility of the RCCs in their jurisdictions, any financial losses in the future will be, theoretically speaking, borne by the provincial authorities. That said, this remains a policy intention, as no provincial government has yet been put to test on this. On a related note, there is little sign that the respective provincial governments have matched the central government's 168 billion yuan debt-for-bonds swaps to help get rid of the RCCs' mounting bad debt. A number of Chinese scholars specializing in rural credit had indicated to the author that the matching of funds is sporadic, with wealthy provinces contributing more than poor provinces do.

53   From interviews with RCC managers.

About The Author

Dr. Tan Kwan Hong serves as professor for finance, economics, business, leadership and human resource management. Beyond his involvement as a professor, lecturer and an academic writer, he is also an award-winning corporate trainer and lecturer and has given talks to more than 120,000 people on topics such as leadership, entrepreneurship, management skills, communication skills, persuasion, career management skills and personal peak performance.

Apart from accomplishing his Doctor of Philosophy, Dr. Tan Kwan Hong has 3 Masters degrees, in particular, the Master of Science (Finance) (With Distinction) from Grenoble Ecole de Management, the Master of Science (Human Resource) (With Distinction) from Edinburgh Napier University, and the Master of Education (With High Distinction) from Monash University.

He has also obtained 3 graduate diplomas to supplement his knowledge, in particular, the Specialist Diploma in Business Analytics (With Merit) from Temasek Polytechnic, the Post Graduate Diploma in Business Administration (With High Distinction) and the Graduate Diploma in Training and Development (With High Distinction), both from Aventis School of Management in Singapore. He has scored in the top grade category for all Masters and Graduate Diploma programs, and was the overall top student for several of these programs.

Dr. Tan Kwan Hong first graduated from the Singapore Management University with the Bachelor of Science (Economics) (With Distinction).

As an avid learner, Dr. Tan Kwan Hong has also obtained more than 150 different certifications in the areas of business analytics, finance, human resource, project management and sports science. He is a Certified Business Analytics Specialist (CBAS) and a Certified Associate in Project Management (CAPM). He is also a

Distinguished Toastmasters (DTM), the highest accolade achievable from Toastmasters International, only awarded to less than 1% of all members worldwide.

As a national science champion in his youth, Dr. Tan Kwan Hong was also the recipient of several scholarships, academic and university awards, national awards, public speaking awards, and also has a national-level strategy case competition championship title. He has also represented his country in regional conferences on academic and policy issues.

Dr. Tan Kwan Hong's corporate experience spans strategy consulting, financial research, education management and policy development. He can be contacted at www.tankwanhong.com and www.linkedin.com/in/tankwanhong.